The NEW GAME

MAKING MONEY WHILE YOU SLEEP

WAYNE MALCOLM

www.fast-print.net/store.php

The NEW GAME

Copyright © Wayne Malcolm 2010

www.icancoach.co.uk

ISBN 978-184426-920 4

Cover design & layout by David Springer

First published 2010 by

FASTPRINT PUBLISHING

Peterborough, England.

An environmentally friendly book printed and bound in England by

www.printondemand-worldwide.com

This book is made entirely of chain-of-custody materials

Content:

Introduction

'Nobody talks of entrepreneurship as survival, but that's exactly what it is and what nurtures creative thinking.'
Anita Roddick

Make your choice

Over the next three to five years, you are either going to become very rich or very poor. The choice is yours. Your job is not secure and your currency is losing its value so that your wages may not be able to cope with the rising cost of living. Job losses and inflation are going to throw millions more into unemployment and sudden poverty. For many, this will happen overnight and without warning!

There is something you can do about it but sadly most people won't. They will vote and hope that some politician will take them back to the glory days of job-security. However this will all amount to a waste of time. The only person who can secure your financial future is you. It is not too late but you must take immediate action and go to work on a new game plan for success.

All the statistics show that the rich are getting richer, even in the recession, while the poor are getting poorer. The jobs that were lost are not coming back. The middle class is shrinking and may eventually become extinct. The government may not be in a position to help you because it is in debt to the tune of trillions. Many will become poor overnight if they don't take action now to secure their own futures. This book is about how you can become very rich over the next three to five years.

The Jarrow March (October 1936)

During the great depression, the North East of England suffered immensely when domestic and international trade in steel, coal and shipping collapsed. The boomtown of Jarrow was a prime example. It was a prosperous town at the beginning of the 20th century. More than a quarter of the world's shipping tonnage was built in the North East of England. Virtually everyone had jobs and enjoyed the prosperity of world trade. By the end of the depression the town was hardly recognizable. The plants were closed and the people became poor overnight.

Their protest didn't help either. In an historic attempt to get the government of Westminster to intervene in the closure of plants, over 200 men marched for three hundred miles from Jarrow to Westminster. The march attracted world press and put the government of Britain under immense pressure. When the marching-men got to Westminster their efforts went unrewarded. They were each given £1.00 to catch a train back to Jarrow.

The tragedy is that these industry workers had no other skills and were completely reliant on manual jobs in a plant.

The coal miners

The same tragedy happened during the Thatcher years for the coal miners in England during the mid eighties. These miners went on strike for approximately one year between 1984 and 85 to protest government plans to close 20 pits. The pits were closed and the people became poor overnight. In spite of government schemes to re-skill these workers, those towns have never recovered from the devastation.

History repeats itself.

Since the recession of 2008, whole towns in Britain and America have gone the way of Jarrow. Their manufacturing plants and key industries have closed down and the people have become poor overnight. The reason why the plants and pits closed in previous recessions is that it no longer made any economic sense to keep them open. Economic sense is likewise the reason why many more plants, industries and towns are going the way of Jarrow. The world has changed and a new economic era has arrived. Those who insist on cleaving to the past may find themselves face to face with poverty sooner than they think.

Lehman Brothers

Lehman, once the world's fourth-biggest investment bank, filed the biggest U.S. bankruptcy in September 2008 with assets of $639 billion. It fired more than 13,000 U.S. employees from mid-2007 through October 2008. When Lehman Brothers of London let go of 5000 employees, it all happened in one day without notice. 5000 people went to work only to find out that the company had gone into administration and that they were now jobless.

Citigroup

The Independent reported the following concerning the Citi-banking group:

Tuesday, 18 November 2008

'Citigroup, the ailing US financial giant, shocked the market yesterday by announcing that it would cut 52,000 jobs by the second half of next year. The planned 15 per cent cut in staff numbers comes on top of 23,000 jobs already axed since the bank's employee numbers peaked at the end of last year and are designed to cut costs by 20 per cent to about $50bn (£33.3bn). The bank warned that London and New York would inevitably bear the brunt of job cuts.'

In the US alone, manufacturing industries have shed over 212,000 jobs in the past year. The Financial Services industry has shed over 79,000 in the past year. And that's only two industries. Most of the victims are job-dependent and have no way of generating an income without a job. How would you cope without a job?

The Samson effect

The Biblical story of Samson ends with a dramatic sequence of events. In the closing scene, Samson is standing between two pillars within arms reach of each other. These two pillars were the supporting pillars upon which the entire facility leaned. He then proceeded to push on the pillars until they gave way. The result was that the whole structure came down and everyone in it was killed. The structure was a temple for worship. The congregants had gathered to celebrate their success and prosperity. They were celebrating just moments before the whole structure came crashing down on their heads.

The parallels between then and now are striking. Our economy is likewise resting on two pillars. The first pillar is the pillar of job security. The second is the pillar of borrowing. Our entire system and way of life is based on the idea of job-security and borrowing from banks. Unfortunately for those who lean on them, it is these very two pillars that have moved and are giving way right now! The implications for society are huge because they call into question our very way of life.

What would you do if you lost your job? What if you couldn't get another one? What if your bank withdrew your overdraft or if you couldn't get credit?

None of these scenarios are unrealistic. They have happened to millions in just two years since 2008. As a result, millions have lost their homes, their savings and their dreams. If you are not one of those to whom this has already happened, you should at least wake up to the fact that it could be you next.

With our very way of life under question, we are now forced to look for alternative ways to support ourselves and to secure our futures.

The great illusion

The temple in our metaphor represents the illusion of success that has been embraced by the middle classes and that is sold to us by the schools. It is this illusion that is crumbling around us every day. The record number of Job losses, home foreclosures, bankruptcies and defaults are only the beginnings of a crumbling illusion. *It is an illusion to think that you own anything that is purchased with borrowed money.* Especially when the terms of the borrowing (usually concealed in small print), give the lender a first charge over all your assets.

The congregants in this metaphor are the middle classes. This is the group who are caught up in the great illusion of borrowed success. With their secure jobs they qualify for borrowing and with the help of credit cards, store cards, buy now & pay later schemes, loans, overdrafts and mortgages they have convinced themselves that they are doing well and that life is great. The problem is that the whole illusion is resting on two pillars; a secure job and a lending bank! If these two were suddenly removed then so would the house, the car, the luxuries, the lifestyles, the vacations and the toys that sustained their illusion.

Our way of life!

Our very way of life is sitting on the two pillars of job-security and debt. We send our children, like raw materials, into State controlled factories called schools. These factories are designed to mass-produce a workforce for the public (government) and private (business) sectors. They are not designed to produce entrepreneurs; they exist to create good employees. That is why we all come out of the schools as helpless job-dependents who immediately begin the process of selling ourselves to employers in exchange for just enough to pay our debts. Once employed, we are expected to hold on for dear life and hope that the job will last.

With a secure job we quickly qualify for borrowing and are immediately targeted by the banks and financial institutions who are prepared to lend us the money needed to create the illusion of success. The house, the car, the furniture, the holidays, the leisure and the lifestyle are all made available to good employees through credit cards, store cards, loans, overdrafts and mortgages.

Few jobs pay you enough to create real success however if the job pays you enough to service your loans, which are supporting and sustaining your lifestyle, then it is considered a good job.

This way of living is so engrained into the fabric of our culture that most people can't even imagine that an alternative exists. It is simply the way the world works and it is only the fools who question it.

Inception

Unlike previous generations, the State and Industries cannot force people to work for them using violence or physical coercion. Today, those in search of a cheap workforce must convince people to volunteer for the role.

The block buster movie **Inception** is all about planting a thought in someone else's mind in such a way that they think it is their own. I cannot think of a better way to describe why it is that the masses have volunteered for a role that makes them totally dependent on a job and on a debt.

Why would anyone in their right mind volunteer to become part of a cheap workforce that is designed to make their employers rich? The answer is that no one told them that an alternative exists and that they have a choice. The ruling classes know that if they can convince the masses that working for them is the only option available, then the masses will volunteer to abandon their own pursuits of wealth and instead commit forty years of their life to making someone else wealthy.

Job-security is dead!

There is no such thing as a secure job in the modern world. A good job – yes! A great job – Yes! But a secure job - No! It use to be that you could hold down a job for life and then retire in your 60's with a golden carriage clock and a pension. However, today the average person can fully expect to have between 10 and 20 different jobs in 5 different career-sectors throughout the course of their working life.

The only person who can guarantee you a job for life is you! To look for job security anywhere else is indicative of an old-game mindset and a failure to come to terms with the new world.

A new era is here!

We are at the dawn of a new economic era in which there are going to be big winners and even bigger losers. The big winners will be those who take full responsibility for their own financial futures and who have the courage and determination to create their own sources of income. The even bigger losers will be those who are patiently waiting for a politician to bring them back to the industrial age of job security. The bad news is that most people are going to lose because they will procrastinate, speculate, hope and vote until it is simply too late to reverse the effects of their indecisive actions. They are going to get poorer and poorer as the years roll by and will become increasingly dependant on a broke State in order to survive.

The credit crunch, job losses, cuts in public services, inflation and home foreclosures are unfortunately only the beginning of sorrows for the mis-educated masses who were programmed to become job-dependent, debt-dependent and State-dependent.

Good news

The good news is that you don't have to be one of them if you take action now! This book is a wake up call for anyone who will heed its core message. It offers an alternative strategy and game plan for those who don't want to be in the temple when the great illusion comes crashing down.

The old game of job security is now obsolete. Great jobs are still available and will be for centuries to come, however they are not secure! No employer can guarantee you a job for life; neither can they guarantee you a pension when you retire. They can't even guarantee that they will be in business this time next year. Even if you apply new rules to the old game, you may still lose in life. Playing the old game even harder is also a recipe for disaster because no matter how hard you work; jobs are no longer secure, the banks are scared to lend and the economy is unpredictable.

It is not the rules that have changed; it is the game! The new economic era has created a new game based on new rules, a new mindset and a new set of skills. The new game is entrepreneurship and for the first time in history, it can be played by anyone who knows the rules and acquires the skill-set necessary to succeed.

This book will teach you how to become an independent entrepreneur. You will learn how to locate or create money sources that continue to pay you long after the initial work is done. You will also learn how to create multiple income sources so that you are never reliant on a solo income. Finally you will learn that business processes can be outsourced and automated in such a way that they continue working for you while you sleep.

Some people will take exception to my subtitle, *'making money while you sleep'* because it flies against everything they believe about making money. They don't understand that making money while you sleep is the objective of every true entrepreneur. The entrepreneurs are not trying to create for themselves another job. They are not even interested in running a business. They are trying to create multiple money sources or systems that continue working for them while they travel, play sports, raise families and take breaks. They understand that it may take years to achieve this but that doesn't alter the objective.

The new **GAME** is about:

- Generating
- Alternative
- Money sources through
- Entrepreneurship

Alternative incomes are imperative for people who realize that the great illusion is crumbling. So are multiple incomes for those who want to enjoy a better quality of life. The great news is that multiple incomes does not equal multiple jobs. This book explains why the main job of smart entrepreneurs is making money while you sleep!

Chapter 1

The Old Game

*'You cannot build character
and courage by taking away a man's
initiative and independence.'*
Abraham Lincoln

Compulsory State education in the modern world has a well-documented history. Europe's first national system of education was set up by King Fredrick William I of Prussia (Germany) in the 1700s. King Frederick William III, who suffered a humiliating defeat during the Napoleonic wars, was later faced with the dilemma of maintaining order in his kingdom without the use of his military.

His advisors suggested that he could strengthen the State's hold on society by increasing the powers of the school system. Children between the ages of 7 and 14 had to attend a State run school. Parents could be fined or have their children taken away if they did not attend. The objective was to strengthen the States hold on society by churning out obedient subjects and loyal soldiers.

This was a win-win for both parents and the State. Parents got their children educated for free, whilst the king had a chance to indoctrinate these children. The children were rewarded for obedience and punished for disobedience. They were taught unquestioning loyalty to the King and service to the country. It worked; the nanny state raised all the children and groomed them for a life of service to the King.

Little has changed since King Frederick. The school system is still designed to churn out workers. They are like factories who specialize in the mass production of a workforce for the ruling classes.

John Gatto

John Gatto, is a veteran school teacher with over 30 years experience in schools from differing social brackets. He taught in the inner-cities as well as in the suburbs of New York. He has in fact been named teacher of the year several times over. However, John Gatto is perhaps the most outspoken critic of the public school system.

He argues persuasively in his many books that the school system exists to create workers for governments and industries. He calls it a weapon of mass instruction designed to benefit the State and not society.

Cast your mind back to your own school years or even look over your child's shoulder. You will notice that the rewards and punishments are all based on obedience and not on intelligence. You were taught how to sit, listen, work hard and obey your teachers without question.

If you did this, you were rewarded with ticks and stars. If you didn't, then you were punished with frowns, detentions and red ink.

                    www.newgamerevolution.com

Mis-education

Unfortunately, no alternatives to employment are taught in schools. In spite of the fact that 99% of the self-made rich have created their wealth through entrepreneurship, this subject is not part of the curriculum in any serious sense. The fact is that if you are going to be rich and financially independent you are going to have to run your own business. However, starting and growing a business is not taught in schools. Except in business studies where people learn just how complicated and expensive starting a business is.

Many business courses do little more than convince a student that they can't start a business. All the business models and strategies taught are based on borrowing from banks. The courses do not encourage self-employment or business ownership. Instead they are designed to prepare you for a corporate role while the entire process is designed to make you attractive to employers.

The 40-year plan

If it sounds like I'm against schools, I am not! I am against the philosophy that guides them. For many people, school is nothing more than a sales pitch in which a 40-year life plan is sold to students. The 40-year plan involves giving 40 years of your life to an employer in exchange for just enough to service your loans. This plan is sold so vigorously that most students come out of the whole experience believing that this is the only option available to them.

No wonder crime rates are so high in urban centers. Most of the gangsters and criminals that terrify our neighborhoods were little angels in primary school. They get to secondary school and everything changes. No doubt there are a number of contributing factors to this phenomenon however lets not pretend that school has nothing to do with it.

Remember, people can only choose from the options that are available to them. These kids were sold a forty-year life plan that is relatively unattractive in the first place. They are then told that if they do well at school, they will become more attractive to better employers and eventually land a good job with great pay. They are also threatened with the prospect of a bad job or worse yet, no job at all if they don't do well at school.

If these kids fail at school (usually a failure to obey orders and not an indication of their intelligence) they become convinced that the 40-year plan won't work for them. Their minds then automatically start looking for alternative ways to make money and to survive and, of course, alternatives exist in the world of crime.

What if those kids were taught: go for the job you want but if you don't get it, then create your own job through self-employment and entrepreneurship? Would that make a difference to crime rates? I think so! Most young criminals that I have worked with (as a counselor) would love to own their own legitimate business. They just don't think they can and have had no training in that department. Contrary to popular opinion, they don't love the gangster life, they hate dodging cops and bullets, they hate hiding money and wish they could make it in the real world.

Age 25-65

The forty-year plan runs from age 25 to 65 in which you are expected to create wealth for your employer from 9-5, Monday to Friday with overtime and occasional weekends. If you work hard on creating your employer's wealth, then you will get paid just enough to service your own debts i.e. house, car, furniture, school fees, luxuries and holidays. This is called the old game and it is fast fading for smart people who have had enough of this legalized form of slavery and covert exploitation.

The great news is that an alternative plan does exist. It has existed for some time now however the schools have refused to teach it.

The reason they have refused is that it doesn't produce job-dependent workers. Instead it produces smart entrepreneurs who realize that business is not as complicated as the schools made it out to be and that the alternative to employment is self-employment not unemployment.

The alternative plan is what I call the new game. It is the smart alternative for people whose jobs are uncertain or who have been laid off. Many people think that playing the old game of job-security by a new set of rules will be enough to sustain their illusions, however the economy has changed so fundamentally that the old game doesn't work even if you apply new rules to it.

It is not the rules that have changed, it is the game! We are at the dawn of a new economic era in which the new rules only work for people who are playing the new game.

Chapter 2

The New Game

*'I wanted to be an editor or a journalist,
I wasn't really interested in being an entrepreneur,
but I soon found I had to become an entrepreneur
in order to keep my magazine going.'*
Richard Branson

When under immense pressure (as this generation is),
it is sometimes better to ask yourself; where is this
pressure heading rather than why is this pressure here?
In this sense you can focus on what you are going towards
rather than on what you are going through. When you consider
the financial squeeze placed on individuals and industries, the
question to ask is; what is this pressure forcing me to do?
The answer is that it is forcing you to generate alternative
streams of income.

Alternative incomes?

Over the next few years, millions of people are going to
experiment with running a home-based business on the side
in an attempt to supplement their income or to create new
income streams all together. Of course they will try to find new

jobs at first, however when the penny drops, they will quickly realize that it might be easier to create a job than to find one.

Once employers realize that they can run a profitable business with fewer staff and lower costs, they are never going to go back to the waste and excess that marked the boom years of easy borrowing. This means that jobs are going to be harder to find and harder to keep than ever before. Those who do manage to keep a job will be asked to do more hours for less pay and will work under the sword of their employer's scrutiny and discretion.

This sort of pressure is creating a new economic era in which ordinary people are being forced to make additional money or to create their own incomes in order to stay afloat. I call it the age of the independent entrepreneur.

This new breed of entrepreneurs is quite different from the traditional one's in the following ways:

1. The traditional entrepreneur takes business plans to the bank in order to borrow money for a new business venture. The independent entrepreneur, on the other hand, doesn't need a loan in-order to start a business venture because they have low startup costs and minimal overheads.

2. The traditional entrepreneur needs premises, furniture, equipment and staff in order to start a business venture. However the new entrepreneur uses virtual services and outsources staffing on a cost per sale basis. This means that they only ever pay for a service when a customer pays them.

3. The traditional entrepreneur manufactures or imports/exports bulk items for sale. However the new 'home-based' entrepreneur sources suppliers from around the world who are prepared to drop ship items direct to their customers. This means that the entrepreneur never has to stock products. They simply take orders then contact the supplier.

4. The traditional entrepreneur uses expensive and imprecise methods of marketing. Everything from TV adds and sponsorships to newspapers and magazines. These methods are like a shotgun spraying pellets everywhere in the hope that one will hit. However the new entrepreneur understands that buyers have become communities of connected people through the Internet and is able to join that community as a credible adviser and friend.

The vision and the vehicle

Most people have dreams but very few of them have goals. The difference is that the one constitutes a wish, while the other demands a plan. The truth is that dreams only ever come true for the people who wake up and go to work on them. So what is your dream?

The fact that you have a vision for your life doesn't make you that much different to anyone else in the modern world. We all have aspirations and hopes for a better and more prosperous future. We all want to retire young and retire rich so we can spend more time with our families and friends. In this respect we have moved from survival thinking to quality of life concerns. We are a generation that wants to be healthy, wealthy and happy.

The question is, do you have a suitable vehicle for your vision? In other words, have you identified a career that can deliver to you the dreams that you cherish? Is there a career path that enables you to retire young and retire rich? If your current job is a suitable vehicle for your vision, then work at it as hard as you can. If however you realize that your job can only ever deliver enough for you to pay the bills, then its time you woke up and started doing something else on the side.

Waking up means three things:

You must wake up to the fact that:

- Most of your future dreams are currently being lived out by business owners and entrepreneurs
- The proven way to wealth is to run your own business
- No one is serious about creating wealth that is not equally serious about running a successful business

The people who are currently living your dreams of financial freedom, time freedom, freedom of expression and freedom of mobility are in fact entrepreneurs. They work for themselves and enjoy multiple streams of income from numerous money sources. You can join them if you know their secrets and their strategies.

Money while you sleep

It must sound ludicrous and deceptive to an employee's mindset to suggest that anyone can make money while they sleep. After all, employees trade time for money. They get paid for the hours they give to an employer. No hours equals no pay for most of our workforces. However they should stop to notice that their boss makes money whilst sleeping because he/she has created a system that delivers goods and services to consumers even when the boss is on holiday.

A good business works while the boss is away. This is because the business is ultimately a machine or mechanism for making money. The premises, the equipment and the staff are all components in this machine. Admittedly, for the first few years the boss is actively and tactically engaged in the day to day running of the company. However as time goes on and the business turns the corner (becomes profitable), the boss delegates more and becomes the overseer who watches the business to ensure that it is working properly.

The boss can eventually take two and three week vacations, knowing that the company will continue to trade profitably in his/her absence. The boss may even decide to sell the company as a profit-making machine (staff an all) to the highest bidder. The goal of all business ventures is to make money while you sleep.

This explains why so many new business ventures fail. It is because someone with an employee's mindset started them! It was never their objective to automate their business processes so that it worked for them in their absence. Instead they were simply creating their own job, trading time for money and unable to take a break because the whole system, depends on their daily input.

This way of thinking is a recipe for disaster in the business world because it limits the scope and size of the business to your personal capacity to deliver. If you get sick or have to go abroad, the business simply shuts down until you come back.

Money sources:

The only way to make money while you sleep is to locate or to create a money source. A money source is a mechanism that creates money for you without your day-to-day input. It is your very own ATM machine that dispenses cash as and when you need it.

A money source is like a well. Digging it will take time and effort. However once dug, you have created a water source. Others in the village are now dependent on you for water. They may pay you for it or even work for it. This is the fundamental difference between an employee and an entrepreneur. The employee, works for money but the entrepreneur works to create money sources.

Are you working for a salary or are you working for a source?

Both groups are hard working people. Let's not knock employees. They work very hard, typically a 50-hour week and in some cases more. Weekends and overtime all add up. Over the years employee's hours stack up and amount to one third of their life spent in pursuit of a salary. Back to our metaphor, they work for buckets of water!

Entrepreneurs likewise are hard working people. Sometimes 80 hours a week goes into their business venture. The difference is that the entrepreneur is working hard to create a money machine that works for them while they sleep, take holidays, play golf or work on other ideas. They are not interested in a bucket of water; they want to own the well! They realize that owning a well means that they will never run out of water. Employees on the other hand run out of water (money) each week or each month and have to come back to the owner of the well in order to make some more.

It may take years of hard work to create a money source, but once created, it will feed you for life. The question is, would you rather give one third of your life to an employer in exchange for weekly or monthly buckets of water (money) or would it make sense to spend the next four years of your life digging wells? We'll get to the four-year plan later on.

Multiple income streams

There is a limit to how much you can do in life, but there are no limits to how much you can get done. This means that when you trade your time for money as an employee, your income is limited to the time you have available. However, entrepreneurship is not about doing things; it's about getting things done. Using the four business models that I will give you in this book, you can locate, create and automate multiple money sources, each of which can pay you more than your employer would.

The idea of multiple incomes seems foreign to the mis-educated masses, which were taught to rely on a solo income. A solo income is a bad idea for the following reasons:

- A solo income places you at the mercy of an employer. If you lose your job, you may lose your home, your car and your very way of life. How on earth can anyone consider themselves secure when their entire lifestyle is linked to the thoughts and feelings of another person.

- A solo income limits your options. Many people hate going to work because they are forced to put up with horrid conditions and to work with horrible people. They do it because they have no choice and their options are limited.

- A solo income puts you one step away from poverty. If you lost your job and couldn't get another one, you may be forced to claim government benefits. If you think the government will take care of you then take a walk through a government housing project at night and get a feel for what it is like to live on government benefits. If you get out alive, you will vow never to go back.

The one-job solution is sold to the masses with such vigor and conviction that many people cannot imagine being secure without one. I have friends who make hundreds of thousands per year and yet still have their parents asking them when they are going to get a real job.

Notice the mantra we were all taught at school: work hard, get a good job! Or if you don't work hard at school, then you won't get good grades and you won't be able to get a good job! The problem is that it takes more than a good job to be financially secure in the new world. A good job is the old game; multiple incomes is the new game. Which would you rather play?

Multiple jobs?

Those who are smart know that financial security is only possible through multiple income streams. If one fails then the others can support you while you repair it or create another one.

Unfortunately, the mis-educated masses still believe that multiple incomes mean multiple jobs. This is because they were brainwashed at school to think that money comes from jobs and that if they work hard they will be able to find a good ONE!

The truth is that multiple incomes do not mean multiple jobs. It means locating or creating more than one money source. I think that everyone should have at least 4 income streams or money sources that they draw from. This is possible if you are a part of four business ventures that work without your daily input.

I do not have multiple jobs, but I do have multiple incomes. My only job is minding my own business! My business has branches and each branch brings me money. Each branch bears fruit that my customers enjoy and each branch works for me while I sleep!

The four-year plan

There is an alternative to the forty-year plan that is sold vigorously to us throughout our school years. However, the plan only works for those people who have totally rejected the forty-year solution.

If working for someone else until you are 62 is an option in your mind, then you probably won't succeed at the alternative plan.

The alternative plan is a four-year plan and it involves four years of hard work as an entrepreneur. The difference is that you will work to create money sources as opposed to working for money. Four years is ample time to create several money sources even if you are working at it part-time to start with.

I should point out that the four-year plan is not a retirement plan. It is a cycle that may need to be repeated several times before you finally retire. It does however allow you to enjoy several mini-retirements throughout your working life. Mini-retirements i.e. one or two years off are a much better solution to the retirement gamble that is sold to us at school.

The mis-educated masses are working towards a final retirement or pension plan. Even their investments are guided by this philosophy. This amounts to gambling with high stakes for the following reasons:

- There is no guarantee that you will live to see your retirement.

- There is no guarantee that your health will allow you to enjoy your retirement

- There is no guarantee that the people you wish to enjoy your retirement with will even be here.

- There is no guarantee that your company will be able to pay your pension.

- There is no guarantee that the government will be able to pay your pension.

- There is no guarantee that your insurance company will still be in business when you reach retirement age.

- There is no guarantee that inflation will not have reduced the purchasing power of your retirement package.

In spite of all these uncertainties, we are all following the piper to the cliff edge of financial disaster. The answer is to reject the forty-year plan and schedule several mini-retirements throughout your working life and to acquire assets that can be liquidated during the years of your incapacity.

Chapter 3

The Four-Year Plan

*'Only free men can negotiate;
prisoners cannot enter into contracts. Your freedom
and mine cannot be separated.'*
Nelson Mandela

Although the four-year plan seems ludicrous to the mis-educated mind, it is a viable and realistic alternative to the forty-year slave trade promoted in schools. In fact, it has produced more millionaires than any other financial plan to date.

A millionaire?

There are four types of millionaires in the real world as follows:

> **A liquid millionaire –** This person has in excess of £1m in the bank and is free to spend it at leisure. The problem is that if they have exactly £1m and then spend £1.00, they are no longer a liquid millionaire! If they buy a dream house or a dream car with it, they can no longer be considered a liquid millionaire.

A paper millionaire – This person owns company stocks that are valued at £1m or more. The problem facing this millionaire is the volatile nature of the stock market. We have all seen stocks crash over night with billions wiped of the value of companies in moments.

An asset millionaire – This person owns real estate or a business that is worth in excess of £1m. Unfortunately these millionaires are often unable to live the millionaire life because their wealth is tied up in assets. I have known some who appeared quite poor even though they owned several properties with a combined value of over £1m. I have also met people in this business who deceptively called themselves millionaires even though their properties were bought with 90% and in some cases 100% mortgages.

A virtual millionaire – This person owns several money sources that generate enough passive income for them to live the millionaire lifestyle. By the way, it really doesn't cost a million to live like a millionaire. In fact you can live 'large' and enjoy the finer life for much less than most people think. If for example, you made £40k per month from a range of money sources, you would be able to live much 'larger' than most millionaires. Although £40k per month sounds impossible to the mis-educated mind, it is the same as 1000 people giving you £40.00 per month for membership in a club or association.

This is a realistic goal within a 12 to 18 month window. All you would need is a hungry market, a killer product and an irresistible offer.

This book offers four business models, each of which have the potential to make you a virtual millionaire within 4 years. So here goes....

Year 1 – The year of transformation!

It is a known fact that 90% of new business ventures fail within three years. What is more shocking is that the reasons for failure are equally well known. In his ground-breaking book, **'The e-myth,'** Michael Gerber explains this phenomenon in detail. His basic claim is that most new business ventures are undertaken by technicians who have a technical skill but no business strategy or systems.

These technicians (i.e. someone who can bake cakes or paint nails), fail to realize that the skills necessary to run a business are an entirely different skill-set than those needed to bake cakes or to paint nails. When going into business, they quickly find themselves out of their depth and drowning in a sea of paperwork, inventory, regulations and management.

In short, Michael concludes that the right mind-set and the right-skill set must precede the start up of a new business venture. This is why, the four-year plan starts out with a gap-year in which your main aim and goal should be to acquire a new mind-set and a new skill-set. Self-development is the master key to professional success. Without it you are simply wasting your time when it comes to wealth creation.

Much was made of the book called, 'The Secret'. It inspired millions to begin attracting good things into their lives by focusing on them with their thoughts. Although the law of attraction is a powerful meta-physical principle, it does not provide an adequate explanation for the success of the self-made rich. Whilst not knocking the book, I would like to let you in on another secret. It is this; your success in life is a reflection of your skills!

There is no spiritual, metaphysical or philosophical substitute for skills! However when the right mindset meets the right skill-set, then success is the inevitable outcome. Mindset alone cannot deliver your dreams to you. You can attract opportunities and personalities into your life through a positive mental attitude and by focusing on the things you really want. However those same opportunities and personalities will quickly walk away from you if your skill-set doesn't match your mindset.

It has been said that 'luck' occurs when preparation meets an opportunitiy. The law of attraction can bring you opportunities but only self-development will render you ready when those opportunities knock on the door. Most people wait until opportunity knocks before making preparations to succeed. This is a terrible mistake because opportunity waits for no man. The only opportunities that will ever benefit you in life are the one's that you are prepared to seize.

I therefore recommend that the first year of your four-year plan be devoted to self-development in three specific areas:

1. **Personal skills:** These include both the intra-personal skills for self-mastery like; emotional intelligence, self-coaching, time management and a positive mental attitude, as well as the inter-personal skills like; negotiating, communications, public speaking and leadership. These skills will serve you well as you embark

on a four-year plan to become a virtual millionaire from multiple incomes.

2. **Modern Marketing Techniques:** These include network marketing, relationship marketing, Internet marketing and social media marketing. Modern marketing is much cheaper than traditional marketing, much more flexible and much more accurate. With modern marketing techniques, you literally get more for less, more exposure for less money, more prospects with less hassle and more sales with less selling. Large companies now recognize the fact that one quarter of the worlds population is online and are now paying consultants hundreds of thousands of dollars and pounds to implement a modern marketing strategy using the Internet and social media. If you master the art of modern marketing, you can use it to accelerate any business venture that you undertake.

3. **Niche research:** Finally you should identify some hungry markets. These are need-to-know, need-to-have and need-to-be consumers of particular products and services. Gary Halbert, the famous marketer once told a class of students that he could sell more burgers than all of them put together, even if they had a superior product and more money for advertising. He said that the only thing he would need in his favor is 'a hungry crowd.'

Many would-be entrepreneurs fail here by failing to study their markets carefully and thoroughly. They have forgotten the fundamental rule of marketing, i.e. the law of supply and demand!

Supply and demand

The law of supply and demand is the fundamental rule for marketing and the guiding light of the successful entrepreneur. This rule says, never sell anything that is not in demand. It also says, find out what people want and then give it to them. If you supply what your market demands, then you will never go out of business.

Consumer behavior and market trends are like a river. They are in a constant state of flow, fluctuation and change. This is why you have to study a business venture carefully before embarking on it. You want to know that your market is buying and not dying. You want to pitch your business where the customers are going and not where they have been. You must have empirical data to prove that the products or services you offer are in hot demand and that they will continue to be in demand for the foreseeable future.

Your personal development plan

To make the most out of your year of self-development, you should start out with a personal development plan (PDP). This is a self-directed and self-managed curriculum of studies. Here's how it works:

You should give four months to each of the three areas for self-development. That's four months on developing your personal skills, four months on modern marketing techniques and four months to niche research. Identify a suitable time and place to study at least one hour per day and two hours per day at weekends. With that in place you should make these seven decisions:

1. Decide to become a speed-learner by studying a range of speed learning techniques including,

speed-reading, mind-mapping and advanced memorization techniques. If you do this in month one, it will set you up for a successful year of learning.

2. Decide to read the equivalent of one book per-month in each of your three areas. Four books on self-development, four books on modern marketing and four books on your niche. The equivalent of a book means that it may take the form of:

- Physical books
- Audio books
- eBooks
- Reports
- Articles
- Academic studies and papers
- Webinars
- Video courses etc

3. Decide to build a library of books, audios, videos, articles, reports and eBooks in each of these three areas.

4. Decide to attend seminars and workshops around these critical subjects.

5. Decide to join associations and networks that embrace these ideas.

6. Decide to subscribe to publications in these fields (both online and offline) and join the mailing lists of mentors, coaches and gurus who teach and train on these subjects.

7. Decide to form or join a master-mind group to discuss each of these subjects weekly.

The master key:

True learning does not occur as you read, listen or watch, it occurs as you write, teach and do. This is because learning occurs on the exhale! Reading, listening and watching are all ways of taking in or inhaling new information. However, thanks to breakthroughs in the science of learning, we now know that the information is only absorbed as you exhale it through writing, teaching and doing it.

It is not the information you take in that changes your life; it is the information that you put out.

If all you do is read books and attend seminars, you may find after a year that you are none the wiser. However if you write articles, teach what you are learning to others and practice the techniques, you will come out of the year a genius.

Start by writing a paragraph summary of every chapter you read. In fact you should get in the habit of summarizing everything you read, listen to or view in your own words.

Years two through four!

Your year of self-development and accelerated growth are critical to the success of your four-year plan because it will give you the intellectual capital and edge necessary to launch successful business ventures. Throughout years two to four, you should continue learning even if the pace slows down. Determine to continue reading the equivalent of a book a month and continue to attend seminars and events that pertain to your niche. Keep your subscriptions live and stay abreast of trends and forecasts in your chosen niche markets.

Year two – The year of implementation

Year two of your four-year plan is all about implementation. You are now ready to start your first business venture using nothing more than intellectual capital. I highly recommend the middle-man model for your first venture for the following reasons:

1. There is usually no financial outlay necessary for you to become a middleman because the whole model relies on selling third party goods and services as an agent, affiliate or associate.

2. There is no need to manufacture or to fulfill product orders when you are a middleman because you simply represent an existing company. Your main job is marketing, sales and negotiating deals. Once an order is placed, your job is done and the commissions flow in your direction.

3. The middleman model can make money for you while you sleep if you negotiate long-term contracts and continuity programs. E.g. if your middleman business has to do with car sales, then you will only get a kick back when a car is sold.

   On the other hand, if your middleman business involves car rentals and leases, then you can negotiate big contracts with big firms whose hiring needs are vast and permanent. This deal should pay you a commission on every vehicle rented or leased for the duration of the deal.

We will cover this business in detail in the next chapter.

Once your middleman business has been set up and a few deals are in the bag, you should prepare to launch your military business model. The military model involves raising up an army of sales people to sell products and services for you. This business opportunity is typically available through multi-level marketing (MLM) companies.

I highly recommend that you seize an MLM opportunity for the following reasons:

1. The outlay for starting the business is usually low and typically covers the costs of training and tools for your job.

2. MLM companies are usually committed to training and motivating agents in all aspects of sales and relationship marketing.

3. The MLM business relies on recruiting and motivating a sales force. The environment is usually charged with ambition and passion for the product and the mission. The training alone is a good reason why you should seize an MLM proposition in your year of implementation.

Of course you can start your own MLM company during your year of implementation, however this may be costly and the potential for mistakes is high. A full discussion of the military model exists in the next chapter.

By the end of year two, you should have two income streams from two distinct business ventures i.e. your middleman business and your military model.

Your main goal in year two is to make as much or more money than you make from your job. Your main advantage will be the intellectual capital you will have gained from your year of transformation.

Year 3 – The year of acceleration

Your year of acceleration is the year that you pull out all the stops and take entrepreneurship to the next level. Your year of transformation and implementation should have convinced you that real money can be made as an independent entrepreneur. Now you are ready to accelerate your efforts and become a full-time entrepreneur as follows:

1. Consider going full time as an entrepreneur. Of course this should only be a consideration if you achieved your goal in year 2 of making as much or more money from your business ventures than you did on your job. If you were able to make more money from your middleman and military business than you did on your job, on a part-time basis, then imagine what you could make if you went full time into the business of locating and creating money sources.

2. Convert your middleman business into a full-blown brokerage. E.g. if your middle man business involved securing clients for an accounting firm, then simply make the same deal with a variety of accounting firms and position your company as an accounting brokerage. This means that you can expand the business by offering the right deal to different sorts of client.

3. Decide to multiply the size of your sales force and to triple your income from sales. If your team of 12 people each recruited 12, there would be 144 people in your team or down line. If they each sold a continuity program worth $40.00 per month to you, then you would be earning $5760.00 per month. Offer bonuses and incentives to your team, give them a name for identity (i.e. the dream team or team conquest) and otherwise inspire them to reach their own sales targets.

4. Incorporate your companies. The benefits of a corporation are numerous when it comes to taxation and profits. Keep your companies separate and distinct, even if they are subsidiaries of a parent company.

5. Outsource services and build a dream team. You will now need a virtual office, a virtual PA, a call centre, an accountant and more. Outsource these functions and convince others to join your team on a cost per-sale basis.

6. Set up the other two business models outlined in this book i.e. your mentoring business and your membership business. The mentoring business is an information empire that supplies need-to-know information to a specific niche market. There is more on this in the next chapter. Your membership business may take the form of a club, society, association or fraternity. It offers a range of services and support to a very specific niche group. The benefits of membership must be real if people will pay to join. If it costs

$100.00 per year to be a member of your group, then what would happen if you recruited 1000 members worldwide? You got it, you would grow $100,000 dollars just from your membership subscriptions alone.

7. Implement an Internet marketing and social media strategy for your group of companies. Each should have its own website that is fully optimized for search engines as well as a blog and a presence on major social networks. Drive traffic to your sites and build a massive mailing list of prospects for your businesses.

Year 4 – The year of automation

In year 4 you can realize the dream of making money while you sleep by setting all of your business ventures on auto-pilot. This is where the dream team of committed individuals and the world of virtual services comes in. You should and can, automate all the key functions of your businesses by out-sourcing them on a cost per-sale basis or by hiring support. In the end, you want to reduce your working hours to 4 hours per week. If you don't believe this is possible, then read 'The 4-hour work week' by Timothy Ferriss

You also want to limit your role to the things that you do best and that you most enjoy. The thing you will not get away from is management and leadership. You will have to become a 'one-minute manager' and a strategic leader in order to sustain your enterprises.

In all, your companies should deliver to you four separate income streams, each of which outweighs what you were earning on the job. You may find that some of your businesses are weak whilst others are strong. That's normal. The key is to

create multiple income streams and never to rely on
one source.

Savings and investments:

Perhaps the most important characteristic of the 4-year plan
is its frugality and delayed gratifications. The temptation for
new entrepreneurs, who actually make money, is to make
immediate improvements to their quality of life. With the new
money comes a new house and a new car as well as new
clothes and accessories. You should delay this gratification as
long as possible and instead begin saving and investing the
money you make.

This will require some financial intelligence, as we are no
longer sure about what constitutes a safe investment. I
highly recommend the 'Rich Dad' brand by Robert Kiyosaki. It
is, in my humble opinion, the most comprehensive financial
education available today. What I can say is that you should
invest your money in assets that yield monthly or quarterly
dividend payouts without losing their value.

You may also purchase a franchise or buy into a growing
company as a senior partner.

Your exit route:

If you do the four-year plan right, you will become a virtual
millionaire and continue making money from your ventures for
several years to come. This is particularly true for those who
watch market trends and are able to adjust their offer to satisfy
consumer demands.

If you can show on paper that your companies are making
significant profits each year and that the systems are fully
automated so that they work without you, then you will be able

to sell those companies to buyers both at home and abroad. It may surprise you how much investors are willing to pay for a company that has a future.

A friend of mine built a computer game while he was at high school. After successfully selling it to fellow students, he sold his little company for $1m.

Tony Robbins (the billionaire life coach) was able to take one of his companies to market for an initial public offering (IPO). This meant that it would become a public company trading on the stock market. He made $400m with an initial public offering.

Who knows, your middleman business or your mentoring company may eventually sell for $5m a piece. Wooo! That sure beats the 40-years of voluntary slavery that we were programmed to embrace at school.

I think you get the picture. The 4-year plan is realistic and viable if you work hard at the things that work!

Chapter 4

Money Sources

*'The entrepreneur is not really interested in doing the work;
he is interested in creating the way the company operates.
In that regard, the entrepreneur is an inventor. He or she
loves to invent, but does not love to manufacture
or sell or distribute what he or she invents.'*

Michael Gerber

Money is a medium of exchange and as such its true
source is the value of the thing you exchange for it. Valuable
information, products or services can all be exchanged for
money if you learn how to package, promote, price and
position them for sale. In short, you get money by giving
value for it. Value is the true source of money. Your job
is to source or to create value and then give it to others
in exchange for money.

This chapter explores four business models that you can use
to give value for money. A business model is effectively a
business strategy that can be replicated and applied to any
number of business ideas. It is called a model because it is
made up of separate components that come together to form
a system. The key is in ensuring that all the right components
are in place. This chapter is about the four business models

that have proven to create wealth for those who employ them. I have chosen these business models for the following reasons:

- Each of them can be run from home

- Each of them can be started with little or in some cases no financial outlay.

- Each of them has the potential become a commercially viable business that can be sold to buyers.

- Each of them has the potential to be automated in such a way that they work independently of your daily input.

- Each business, once fully automated is effectively a low maintenance business. They can be run successfully with minimal input from the entrepreneur that created them.

- Each of them can be applied to any niche market chosen by the owner.

- Each model is flexible and can be adjusted to suit the rapid changes taking place in the markets.

- Each model is based on the real business behind real business.

Real business

Real business occurs at the point of sale. Many companies lost sight of this blatant fact, thanks to easy borrowing and bank interventions. So long as they make enough money to service their loans, they feel secure in the knowledge that lines of credit are readily available. However that has all changed as lines of credit have become more difficult to obtain and banks are less will to lend without iron-clad security.

This is all great news for consumers who have now become the chief priority for companies and industries. They are slowly waking up to the fact that without sales, they are not in business. This is creating the much needed customer orientation and customer care that was missing when credit was readily available.

The purpose of a business is to create and to keep customers. Outside of this outcome there really is no business in progress. You may cook the best food and have the nicest restaurant, however without customers you are not in business. Likewise you may produce the best music, but you are not in the music business until someone buys your music.

Sales is not just the oldest profession on earth, it is the only profession for smart entrepreneurs. Think about it; all businesses depends on sales. There are no homes without sales, no cars without sales, no food in the stores without sales, no music or theatre without sales, no holidays or recreation without sales and no clothes without sales.

In spite of this simple fact, many people are adverse to sales and feel as though it is a profession without dignity or that it is somehow beneath them to sell. They feel uncomfortable asking for money in exchange for food and services. If that's you, then take a good look around you now and try to find one item in your room or on the train that was not conceived, created, marketed and sold by entrepreneurs!

This is simply the way the world works and it would serve you well to deal with the world the way that it is rather than the way you wish it was. The fact is that any idea or item that is of value to humankind is going to be distributed through sales. Thomas Edison invented the electric light bulb, but it was entrepreneurs who decided to put them in every home through sales. Sales makes the process of producing it worthwhile to the producer.

The real business behind real business

Even though real business occurs at the point of a sale, there is a business behind that business. The real business behind real business is marketing. Marketing includes everything that a company does to create awareness, interest and demand for its products and services. It is the collection of activities that generate sales for companies.

There are old ways of marketing as well as new ones. I highly recommend the new ways because they are much cheaper, much faster, much more flexible and much more available to independent entrepreneurs. Smart entrepreneurs don't need huge marketing budgets because they know how to research markets for free and how to position themselves as pillars of specific buying communities. If for example you sell a new blood-sugar monitor for people with diabetes, you can simply join the conversation that is already going on in that community and position yourself as a pillar of that community using an effective Internet and social media strategy. Big companies are just waking up to this fact and didn't notice the revolution in communications that was happening right under their noses.

Each of our four business models relies on the core functions of business, which are marketing and sales. At the same time our business models seek to strip away and even eliminate the expensive excesses and complications that come with traditional business models. So here they are:

Model 1: The Middleman model

I once had a conversation with an accountant who seemed quite intrigued by my seminar business. His eyes opened wider and wider as I told him that I speak to small and large audiences of entrepreneurs up and a down the country. He then disclosed to me that his practice needed to expand and that he would be most grateful if I could recommend him to my entrepreneurs. Of course I quizzed him about the sort of services he offered and proceeded to question his capacity and prices.

Then I hit him with the big question, what's in it for me? How much will you give me for every client I bring your way? I was pleasantly surprised to know that he was prepared to give me between 10 & 20% of client fees for life. *Kerching!*

This was an eye-opener! You see I'm not an accountant, however this gentleman was giving me an opportunity to go into the accounting business as a middleman, making referrals and recommendations to my own networks.

Sitting in one of my seminars was a young man who was part Surinamese. It turns out that his relatives own a gold mine in Surinam and that he was their appointed agent for international sales. He asked if any of my clients were interested in gold? *Kerching!*

I asked him the big question; what's in it for me? And was pleasantly surprised when I found out that he was willing to give me 50% of his own profits for any referrals that resulted in a sale. I'm not a gold merchant, but this guy was giving me an opportunity to become one as a middleman, making referrals and recommendations to my own networks.

Finally, I recently had to hire a luxury vehicle and in no time struck up a friendship with the owner of the company which specialized in luxury vehicles for hire. I'm talking Bentley, Rolls Royce, Ferrari, Lamborghini etc. It turned out that they also hire helicopters, Yachts and other such rich kid toys. He then asked me if I had clients that might be interested – *Kerching!*

I of course asked the big question, what's in it for me? How much do I get? He instantly placed a lucrative offer on the table. I'm not in the luxury car business however this guy gave me an opportunity to go into the business as a middleman, making referrals and recommendations to my own networks.

The middleman model means becoming an agent, associate or affiliate of an existing company whose products and services are of interest to your own networks. Here's how it works:

1. Identify networks, associations, clubs or forums in your chosen niche market and join them. Submit articles, attend events and contribute to discussions (whether on or offline) held on your subject. Build relationships with key individuals and otherwise get yourself known.

2. Identify companies that service this niche with products or services. Ensure that the products or services have continuity programs i.e. they get paid monthly or there is plenty of repeat business.

3. Explain to the company that you are part of a network that utilizes the services they offer and ask for a percentage of any business you put

their way. Ask them for a referral fee and a sales commission. Many companies will pay for quality leads that you generate as well as sales.

4. Once a contractual deal is in place, print a business card and develop a website that positions you as a consultant in that field.

5. Make recommendations and referrals to your network and otherwise promote the services that you offer through your partner company. Ensure that orders are placed through you and that you retain control of the relationship.

Model 2: The military model

This model involves recruiting and training a formidable sales force. They may sell products for you or become part of your team in an MLM company. Napoleon once said, 'I would rather put 1000 men to work than to do the work of 1000 men'. Imagine 1000 people selling your products for you. You can do this by joining an existing MLM company or by starting your own. You can also market your products using affiliates.

Affiliates and associates differ from MLM in that they don't get paid for recruiting; they only get paid for selling products. The problem with many MLM companies is that they quickly become a recruitment business with little emphasis on the product itself. Agents get paid for bringing new recruits into the company and not for product sales. At this point the company is virtually operating a pyramid scheme and pyramid schemes are illegal in most of the developed world.

You should avoid such companies because they are short lived and may damage your credibility in the future. Instead you should ensure that the products themselves are hot and not just the business opportunity. Ensure that the products deliver real value to the end user. Make sure that you feel comfortable and convicted about selling the products.

Here are the keys to making the military model work for you:

- Identify a hungry niche market. That is, a need-to-know, need-to-have, need-to-do or a need-to-be market. Then locate or create a killer product that comes complete with an irresistible offer. Alternatively you should find a fairly new MLM company that is servicing a hungry niche market with its own killer-product range and then simply sign up.

- Document a business plan that explains how sales people can profit from the business. Ensure that the compensation plan is both generous and yet realistic. Present the plan in both written and visual (Power Point) formats. Ensure that your recruits can see how working with you can make them rich. Ensure that they understand the compensation plan and that it feels both realistic and doable.

- Recruit sales people into your business using your documented business plan and then train them on how best to achieve their own goals.

- Ensure that your sales people are resourced and supported by the company. If it is your own killer product, then develop a range of tools that your sales people can use to generate leads and sales. Ensure that they can utilize modern marketing methods involving Internet marketing and social media strategies in order to promote their business.

- Celebrate and recognize results amongst your sales team and use the best motivational techniques to keep your team feeling optimistic and enthusiastic about the business. Factor in bonuses as well as other incentives for great performance.

- Operate as a team by giving your team a name, creating team targets and offering bonuses for team performance.

Imagine you recruited a sales team of 100 people within one year.

This is both realistic and achievable on a part time basis. Now imagine that each of them sold one product per month that generated $20.00 per month for you. You would have created a money source and an income stream worth $2000.00 per month. What is more realistic to imagine is that a hand full will successfully sell 10 or more per month whilst the others average 4 sales. Quite clearly a sales force of 100 people could easily earn you a significant passive income.

Model 3: The mentoring model

The mentoring business model is effectively an information empire that sells need-to-know information to hungry niche markets.

It is otherwise known as the advice or training business and includes a plethora of products and services including:

- Public speaking
- Seminars
- Workshops
- Bootcamps
- Coaching
- Consultation
- Book publishing
- Audio training
- Video training
- eBooks
- Short courses
- Newsletters
- blogging and more...

You may have heard of Tony Robbins, the billionaire life coach or Brian Tracy, the multi-millionaire achievement coach. Maybe you've read something by Les Brown, the multi-millionaire motivator or perhaps you have audio's in your possession from the audio training arm of Robert Kiyosaki's 'Rich Dad' brand. All of these use the mentoring business model to create money sources. Beneath these multi-millionaire information empires are thousands of millionaire coaches, trainers, consultants and info-merchants who, although not as famous, have earned millions by selling their expertise.

This business is perhaps the most lucrative of all the business models because the profit margins are so high. Think about it, these guys sell information and advice! How do you place a value on advice? The answer is that information is only ever worth what it would cost you to not know it and advice is only ever worth the result that your advice delivers.

The information business is ultimately a results business. People only ever buy knowledge and advice because of what they believe they may be able to obtain or avoid as a direct result of that knowledge and advice.

The great news is that the advice business is endless because the same business model can be applied to thousands of niche markets from gardening to parenting, from marriage to divorce and from birth to death. People want advice! This is why the Internet has become the greatest phenomenon of the 21st century because it gives ordinary people access to the greatest library in the history of the world.

Our generation has an insatiable appetite for information unlike any generation before it. The reason we crave information so badly is that our entire way of life depends on it. Our quality of life today is directly linked to what we know. Our progress in life today is limited by ignorance until it is unrestricted by knowledge. This was not always true, but today it is! The difference between the haves and have-nots is a knowledge gap of which the income gap is but an expression.

Today, the difference between a great marriage and rotten relationship is knowledge and skill. Likewise the difference between great health and poor health is often knowledge. The difference between a successful career and a failing one is what the successful person knows that the unsuccessful person doesn't.

Here's how the mentoring model works:

- Identify a buying niche market. This is a need-to-know group of consumers who regularly pay for advice or information. It could be in the area of relationships, careers, finances, faith, politics, business, health, fitness or sports.

- Find out where the pain is in your niche market using online market research tools and questionnaires. Study your prospects intensely to find out what their frustrations, fears and concerns are. Where are they stuck and where does it hurt? You should also become familiar with their goals, dreams and aspirations.

- Locate experts in this area and study their advice carefully. Build a library of books, audios, articles and reports from reputable sources in your field. Translate that advice into your own articles and then submit them to online article directories. You should also set up a blog to post your articles as well as other useful articles that may be of interest to your prospects.

- Decide to achieve expert status in your field by mimicking the advice of established experts. This doesn't happen over night. You should read at least 5 books by established experts in your field before publishing your own articles. It also helps if you have personal experience with your subject. E.g. if your info-empire is going to service the diabetic community then either you or someone close to you must have wrestled with the condition.

- Identify any communities, clubs, associations or forums where your prospects are members and then join them. Get around your prospects, mingle with them and understand their needs. If no forums exist then create one online and lead that community.

- Create a powerful lead generator. A lead generator is a free or inexpensive, yet high value product i.e an audio or an eBook. Offer it free or at a very reduced cost to people who join your mailing list. Decide to build a mailing list of qualified prospects using online methods.

- Use email-marketing techniques to educate your list about the virtues and value of your product range.

- Source or create a plethora of products that address the needs of your niche including: Books, audios, videos, software, seminars, workshops, coaching, ebooks and more. The more products you have is the more money you'll make as an info-preneur! Making info products is relatively easy and inexpensive when you know how.

- Become a public speaker and give talks on your subject. No need to charge for these talks because the trick is to drive the entire room to your back table where audios, books, study guides and other resources are on special offer.

The master key to building an information empire is to build a huge list of qualified prospects. Imagine that you had a list of 50,000 single people who are actively looking for a relationship. Imagine that you email them tips and advice every week. Imagine that you give them free resources every month.

Now imagine offering them an eBook worth $15.00 on 'How to tell if someone likes you!' Now imagine that over the course of a month, 1000 people buy it! Wooo, you just made a cool

$15,000 from only 2% of your list! Typically between 1 and 3% of your list will buy from you.

The membership model will take this concept to the next level! Here goes...

Model 4: The membership model

Based on the last illustration, what if you started a singles network and charged $10.00 per month for membership. Your network offers a safe environment for singles to meet and chat online as well as monthly relationship-coaching audios and eBooks. Now imagine that 1000 people join it from your list of 50,000. You are now headed to make $120,000 per year from your network. Would that help you say goodbye to your job?

The same result is possible with a network of 500 people at $20.00 per month or 50 people at $200.00 per month. Likewise the same result is possible regardless of the subject. It could be politics, parenting, table tennis or cinema. The possibilities are endless for smart entrepreneurs who are in possession of a high quality mailing list. The quality of your list will determine your volume of sales. That's why I don't recommend that you buy a list. I suggest that you build one using online list building techniques.

We are living in an age of networks, associations, clubs and communities. People all over the world are trying to connect and collaborate around their special interests. Thanks to the Internet, you can start up a global community from your home PC. After all that's where Facebook, MySpace, Twitter and other social phenomena started. These networks now have hundreds of millions of members' worldwide.

The great news is that clubs, associations and networks can work in any niche market if:

- Your network, club or association is relevant i.e. it relates to the needs and aspirations of a hungry niche market.

- It delivers real value to members. The benefits of joining your group should be clearly listed in your promotional campaigns.

- You over-deliver and amaze your members with more than they expected to receive.

- Membership is inexpensive and flexible i.e. no fixed term or cancelation fees. Of course this depends on your niche and the value you have to offer. You may for example start an investors club that costs $200.00 per month to join.

- Members are offered incentives for paying annually instead of monthly.

- Members are offered incentives for recruiting new members.

- You use some reverse psychology and limit the number of members or make the joining criteria strict. You can charge more for membership in an exclusive club.

The membership model works best by association. People want to know that important people are members of your association or that they endorse the club. Your job is to convince some important characters to join in or to become patrons and non-executive directors. This may be easier than it sounds. You simply offer them free membership or make some other deal with them that offers them tangible benefits.

Endorsements are equally important. You should seek to display the logos of other key organizations on your website. Again you may have to make a deal with them to secure this privilege.

Finally, the way that you are personally perceived is also important. You should go to work on your bio to make it attractive and impressive. Likewise you should decide to become a master of the subject at hand.

Chapter 5

The Eyes of an Entrepreneur

'The real source of wealth and capital in this new era is not material things.. it is the human mind, the human spirit, the human imagination, and our faith in the future.'
Steven Forbes

'The entrepreneur in us sees opportunities everywhere we look, but many people see only problems everywhere they look. The entrepreneur in us is more concerned with discriminating between opportunities than he or she is with failing to see the opportunities.'
Michael Gerber

The fundamental difference between an employee and an entrepreneur lies in their worldview. Your worldview is the way that you see the world through your own brand of tinted spectacles. Those spectacles are designed to obscure certain things while highlighting others.

What do you notice?

The truth is that we notice what we are subconsciously looking for. Often in my seminars I run a simple competition. I ask the class to look around the room and to take note of everything in it that is colored RED. I then offer a prize to the person who can remember the most items. I tell them that they have 10 seconds that start; now! The students then start looking frantically around the room taking a mental note of everything in it that is colored red. They go for furniture, clothes, accessories, flowers; anything that is colored red. When the 10 seconds is up, I tell them to stop and close their eyes. Now I offer my prize to the first person who can stand up and name 10 items in the room that are colored BLUE!

Shock and horror! They protest; we were looking for red! Exactly, I retort, and because you were looking for red, you never noticed the blue. In fact your mind simply omitted and even deleted anything in the room that is blue.

By asking the class to look for red, and by offering a reward incentive, I had successfully programmed their Reticular Activator. The Reticular Activating System sits at the base of the brain and is responsible for deciding what information should be brought to your attention and what information should be discarded as irrelevant. Billions of bytes of information are streaming through your five senses all the time, however we don't notice them because our reticular activating system doesn't deem them relevant. For example; you are probably unaware of what is going on in your left shoulder right now! However, now I've said it, you may notice that sensations exist there.

Your brain is wired to notice what you are looking for and to overlook or obscure what you are not looking for. The whole process is quite sub-conscious and happens at the speed of thought.

Throughout our school years, we are all programmed to look for jobs. We leave school and university as helpless job dependents and immediately begin our search for jobs. We are so wired to notice job opportunities that we fail to notice business opportunities. In this respect, the job-opportunities are RED and the business opportunities are BLUE. We were told by our teachers and parents to look for red. We were offered incentives and rewards for noticing everything in our world that is RED (job-opportunities). However, to our shock and horror, the real rewards in life are reserved for those who notice the BLUE (business opportunities).

To the employee mind-set, the world is in crisis because there are fewer jobs available and because the government is broke. But to the entrepreneur mind-set, the world is in transition and will soon enter an age of unprecedented prosperity in which millions will become millionaires. Although this idea sounds preposterous to the mis-educated mind, it is worth noting that more people became self-made millionaires after the great depression than in any previous era.

This is an age of unprecedented opportunity for the people who have an entrepreneurial world-view. Entrepreneurs notice opportunities because they are looking for them. Of course, if you have more money, then you may notice the more expensive opportunities that promise to deliver millions and billions in rewards. However even if you are broke and have no money, you will still notice an abundance of business opportunities surrounding you if you look for them.

In fact, there are more business opportunities in the world today than there are job vacancies. However this is only clear to the entrepreneurs who are looking for them.

Business to consumer

There are eight major concerns of people living in the modern world. They are:

- Spirituality
- Health & fitness
- Love and marriage
- Careers
- Personal finance
- Lifestyle
- Personal development
- Contribution through charity or politics

These eight each constitute consumer markets in which goods, services and information are sold to the tune of trillions of dollars per year. People spend serious money on these issues. However, when you put each topic under the microscope you will notice that each one houses millions of micro-niche markets. For example in the lifestyle section there are thousands of hobbies that people spend on. Each hobby comes with its own tool kit, its own associations and clubs, its own outfits or dress codes, its own events, its own furniture, its own celebrities, its own magazine subscriptions etc. If your hobby is cooking fine foods, then your spend may include cutlery sets, recipe books, membership in a cooking club, courses on cooking, cooking exhibitions and events, subscriptions to cooking magazines and the list goes on.

Each of these markets and micro-niches represent business opportunities for independent entrepreneurs either as a mentor, a middleman, a military sales team or a membership-based club. Each of the four business models can be applied to cooking, stamp collecting, fishing, astronomy, travel, sports or any other lifestyle hobby.

Please don't forget that hobbies are only one aspect of a person's lifestyle. The same principle holds true for travel, fashion, entertainment, music, dinning, nightlife and more. If you ever exhaust the lifestyle market, then jump over to careers or love or personal finances. There are ultimately more business opportunities in the world today than there are jobs.

Business to business

Hopefully, you can see how an independent entrepreneur can cash in on virtually any business to consumer transaction in the world today. What is not always clear is that for every business to consumer transaction that are between 5 and 20 'business to business' transactions that take place first.

From the hen to the house!

If you had eggs for breakfast this morning, you probably bought them from your local store or you ate at a local restaurant. The question is, how did the eggs get from the hen to your house?

If you bought them at a store, then how did they get to the store?

Quite clearly the eggs started out on a farm. The farmer purchased the land, the equipment and the chickens necessary to farm eggs. This means that someone marketed and sold egg-farming equipment to farmers! I wonder if it was the manufacturer or if it was a middleman?

Next the eggs had to be tested, approved, packaged and transported professionally to their point of sale. Have you ever thought of going into the egg packaging business as a middleman? What about the transportation of eggs? Could that be a lucrative business? Of course! Think about it; millions and millions of eggs are being transported every day all over the world. I wonder what percentage of those eggs makes it without breaking. I wonder if a better way of transporting eggs exists. You get the point!

Companies are doing more business with other companies than they are with consumers. Nothing gets to consumers without a plethora of 'business to business' activities and sales. This means that however many business opportunities exist in the B2C world; there are between 5 and 20 times more opportunities existing in the B2B world.

Innovation:

We are always saying to ourself.. we have to innovate. We got to come up with that breakthrough. In fact, the way software works.. so long as you are using your existing software.. you don't pay us anything at all. So we're only paid for breakthroughs.

Bill Gates

Not only are there millions of B2B and B2C business opportunities in the world today but all of the current goods and services that exist are being replaced by new and improved versions. This is even true of information. Old information in every field is being replaced by new information every year. It is estimated that a 10% improvement on an existing product or service literally constitutes a new product or service. The markets will pay for new and improved versions of virtually anything. Think about cars. Sometimes the only improvement made is in the bumper or the trunk. All of a sudden everybody wants the new shape!

This means that all businesses everywhere are up for grabs because of innovation. For example, I am currently using a Mac book pro to type my book. I remember a time when I used a typewriter. The typewriter has since been replaced by the word processor. Technology will ensure that a new and improved version of my Mac book gets released. When it does, guess what, I'll be first in the queue to get the new and improved version. At the same time that I'm buying my new and improved Mac book pro, millions of others will be purchasing from Apple's competitors because of course they will bring out a rival product. Each of these products will rely on middlemen, associates and sales teams to boost their sales.

The Internet

The great news is that the world is now online. Well, a quarter of the world's population to be exact. This means that the new marketers can trade internationally from the comfort of their own homes. Using a computer and a telephone, you can literally set up a consultancy, a brokerage, a sales team, a membership club or a store selling anything to anyone, anywhere at anytime.

All big businesses are going online and they are being closely followed by mid-sized business who are being closely followed by small businesses. The wonderful news is that they are all relying on affiliate programs and third party sales. There has never been more opportunities for individuals to go into business than there are right now thanks to innovation and technology.

The entrepreneur's secret

Entrepreneurs know something that employees don't. It's a secret! I'm not talking about a metaphysical mystery, I'm talking about a guiding principle or philosophy that underpins every business decision made by a successful entrepreneur. If you've ever watched the TV series 'Dragons Den', in which inventors pitch to a panel of entrepreneurs for money in exchange for a slice of their business, you'll notice that the inventor is always shocked when the panel rejects their business idea. They don't get it! They don't understand why the entrepreneurs cannot see the value of their brilliant invention.

The reason they reject it is because they all know the entrepreneurs secret! The secret is based on the fundamental law of economics: i.e. the law of supply and demand. This law says seven things:

1. You should never supply anything that is not in hot demand.

2. You should start with what the market demands and then create the supply rather than starting with your own idea and hoping that the markets will like it.

3. Your market research to determine the demand should be extensive and vast. You should know who and why consumers will purchase from you as well as where they can be located for advertising and promotions. You must have a USP (unique selling proposition) and be able to prove that consumers will favor you over competitors.

4. Your loyalties should lie with the demand side of the market and not with the supply. (Inventors are often obsessed with their own inventions and not with their consumers needs).

5. You should consider the scope of the demand. Entrepreneurs know that only a fraction of the people who want a product will actually buy it. They will therefore not supply anything that is not in hot demand by large numbers of people.

6. You should consider the duration of the demand i.e. how long will people buy this product for. Will they always need it or is it a one-time sale. If the demand is durable or there is continuity i.e. life after a sale, then the business is of interest to an entrepreneur.

7. You should consider the depth of the demand i.e. is there a range of products and services that can be sold along side this product. Can other support-services be sold with this product? Is there an up-sell or side-sell or down-sell opportunity with this product.

Chapter 6

The New Age!

*'Innovation distinguishes between
a leader and a follower.'*
Steve Jobs

We are already living in a new economic age in which the old game is obsolete. The old game of job-security doesn't work. Even if you want a good job and don't want to run your own business, you now have to approach your career like an entrepreneur by considering and treating your many employers as if they were customers of your own personal services company! This means re-positioning your boss by considering him or her to be your client!

Who do you work for?

Even in the job market, you have to think and work like an entrepreneur in order to secure your life-long employability. Entrepreneurship is the new game and those who don't get it will lose it!

You are already working for yourself, you just don't know it yet! Those who do realize that they are in fact working for themselves are taking innovation, marketing and sales into their own workplace and are revolutionizing their companies as intra-preneurs. They are self-motivated, self-educated and self-regulated because they know that they are working for themselves and that their boss is simply their current client.

Of course their bosses wont want to let them go and will often keep them on as consultants long after they have left the company. The difference is an entrepreneurial mindset versus an employee's mindset. The truth is that an entrepreneurial mindset is the only job security available to you in the modern world. It will not guarantee you a life-long job, but it will guarantee your life-long employability. It is the key to succeeding in the new economic age!

Here are the seven characteristics of the new economic age:

1. It is the age of certain and sudden change!

The only thing that is certain in the new economy is that things are changing all the time. Thanks to technology, the media, politicians and banks we are now living in an age of uncertainty. The only way to win in an age of certain change is to be flexible enough to make rapid and continuous adjustments yourself. Entrepreneurs must stay ahead of the curve by watching trends and patterns in order to make quick adjustments that keep their ventures relevant and competitive.

2. It is the age of the individual

Thanks to technology, individuals can now do from home what once could only be achieved by big companies with big budgets and big buildings. For example, years ago, the record companies decided who would become a star. They owned the studios for music production as well as the means of marketing and distributing the records.

Today an individual can produce music at home, market it on media sharing platforms like You Tube and My Space and then retail it through iTunes. The same is true for book publishers who can now write, publish, market and distribute books from home.

Individuals are no longer at the mercy of industries thanks to Microsoft, Apple and the Internet. This trend has created a new breed of independent entrepreneurs who use technology and outsourcing to make personal fortunes while playing big on a small budget.

3. It is the age of transparency

Anyone can find out anything they want to about you or your company at the click of a mouse. Consumers have become communities who are connected through social networks and forums. They often review products and services offered by companies in their field. Any business that is not transparent is going to lose the new game because they are still playing the old game of secrecy and duplicity. Integrity and transparency are no longer added bonuses, they are absolute pre-requisites for business success. If you want to win the new game, then get up close and personal with your customers. Become a relationship marketer by emphasizing relationships over sales.

4. It is the age of recommendations

Consumers trust consumers and not companies. Thanks to corporate corruption and greed, the trust gap between consumers and companies is wider than ever before. Everyone knows that corporate greed, financial mismanagement and government sleeze has caused the biggest financial crisis since the great depression. Millions of job losses and home foreclosures lie at the feet of these three entities.

The end result for consumers is a loss of confidence and a lack of trust.

Advertisers beware! Glossy brochures, corporate sponsorships and expensive TV adds must now take a back seat to good old fashion recommendations. Word of mouth marketing is now outperforming any other form of marketing in the world today because consumers don't trust you! They know that you will say anything you need to say in order to get what you need to get!

For the new gamer, this means that your chief marketing strategy should be to satisfy and amaze your customers until they are ready to recommend you. Customer amazement is a new game strategy.

It means under-promising and over-delivering. It means blowing your customers mind with a 1st class service. It means prioritizing the customer and crowning them as kings!

5. It is the age of networks

What we once considered to be markets must now be considered communities. This is because a large number of consumers belong to niche networks. These include, social networks, forums, associations, clubs and groups. They communicate with each other and make recommendations based on their own experience.

A smart strategy for new-game entrepreneurs is to join those communities and indeed become pillars of them. If a formal network does not yet exist in your niche, then create one and give it away as a gift to your community. If networks exist in abundance, then join them and begin contributing to the many discussions and reviews. Become a light in your community by submitting articles and writing books that offer real help to people in that group. In this way you'll be perceived as a trusted advisor and not a desperate sales person.

6. It is the age of consumer choice

Consumers have more choice today than ever before. Thanks to online shopping, consumers can instantly compare products and prices before deciding to buy. This calls for some new-game thinking. The old-game idea is to differentiate yourself from your competitors in ways that appeal to your customers. Fortunately this is not a complicated science because there are only four things you can do to differentiate yourself from your competitors. You must be better, cheaper, faster or nicer than your competitors in order significantly differentiate yourself.

However, we are in a new age and although some of the old rules may work for old companies, there are a new set of rules for people who are playing the new game. Here is a key new game strategy:

Become an affiliate of your competitors and recommend your customers to them!

This strategy kills two birds with one stone. Firstly, when you recommend another company to your prospect, your prospect feels as though you have their best interests at heart and not simply your own. Secondly, as an affiliate of your competitors you may get cash back for referrals as well as referrals sent to you by them.

Success is a team sport and those who insist on going it alone can never realize their highest potential.

7. It is the age of collaborations

Joint ventures, collaborations and teamwork are critical success factors for new gamers! The old game was all about crabs in a barrel, each trying to get out but none allowed to go first! The idea of competition is so deeply engrained in the psychology of business schools and old-game entrepreneurs that companies fail to see the potential they have as partners working together.

In their attempts to outdo each other they have simply done themselves out of a better deal. I'm not talking about obscuring our differences or losing our identities nor am I talking about creating a monopoly. I simply believe that your business would do better if other businesses in your field were recommending you. I also believe that they would do so if there was a tangible bottom line reason to do so.

The smart new-game entrepreneur is more of a broker than a sales person. They have a financial interest in the success of many other companies in their field and are working for the good of the industry as a whole.

Those independent entrepreneurs who are winning in a big way are leveraging from joint ventures in their field. This is a smart, new-game concept and will serve you well if you employ it at the very beginning of your entrepreneurial journey! There is an African proverb which says: It is better to be the tail of a lion than to be the head of a mouse! This means that it is better to have 10% of something than to own 100% of nothing! Think about it!

Chapter 7

Making Money!

*'We can believe that we know where the world
should go. But unless we're in touch with our customers,
our model of the world can diverge from reality. There's
no substitute for innovation, of course, but innovation
is no substitute for being in touch, either.'*

Steve Ballmer

There is only one legal way to make money on planet earth;
that is **to exchange goods or services for it.** Even if you
are employed, your employer pays you in exchange for your
services rendered. You in turn, help your employer to
get more money in exchange for goods or services sold by
your company.

The opposite is also true; you only ever give your money
to others in exchange for goods or services. In this respect
money is simply a medium of exchange. In fact none
of us really wants more money! Apart from its power of
exchange, it is nothing more than pieces of cheap paper or
digits on a screen. It is the power of exchange that money
delivers which makes it valuable or not.

What you really want is the things that money can buy. This is exactly how all consumers think. When they make money, they immediately begin thinking of all the things they can do with it. They think of things they can avoid and of things they can obtain with it. They start spending it in their minds. Its value is in direct proportion to the things they can buy with it.
Let me ask you a question, which would you rather have, a million Zimbabwe dollars, or a thousand American dollars? I know the answer, but why? Because a thousand American dollars can buy more than a million Zimbabwe dollars!

Money was made to move! It is nothing more than purchasing power. Stagnant money is worthless. It is a pile of paper, until you realise and activate its 'power of exchange.' Even if you put it in a bank, the bank will rent it out in exchange for more money. This is why money is sometimes referred to as 'liquid,' because it flows in one of two directions:

Away from you – This occurs when you purchase things that depreciate in value or that costs more to maintain than it can be sold for or that are beyond your financial means. These liabilities take money away from you and will ultimately limit your purchasing power.

Towards you – This occurs when you offer goods or services in exchange for money. If the goods or services are in demand and are marketed well, consumers will give you money in exchange for them.

Turning the tide

If you are going to successfully turn the tide and get money flowing towards you, you will have to think of something you can sell. Many people go wrong at this point. They start looking for something to sell with their **'sellers'** spectacles on, instead of the **'buyers'** spectacles. Here's what they do:

'They start thinking about products and services that they would like to sell for one reason or another.'

This is a mistake because research and experience has proven that sellers live and think in a different world than do buyers and that, what impresses the seller may mean nothing to the buyer. Consumers view products and advertising in a completely different way than do companies and sales people. These two perspectives are so far apart that the one is alien to the other as follows:

Each group has its own paradigm, language and values as follows:

Consumer Paradigm

The number one thought going through the mind of a consumer is, **'What's in it for me?'** Consumers are selfish, merciless and suspicious of all advertising. They want more for less, they want it now and they want to retain total control even after the purchase!

Seller Paradigm

This is how sellers think: We have a good product, consumers need it and they are crazy if they don't buy it!

Consumer Language

Consumers describe products in terms of benefits to themselves. They speak about the promise more so than the product!

Seller Language

Sellers describe their products in terms of their features, qualities and standards. Color, shape, size, materials, power, specifications etc. They often use trade jargon when talking to customers or when advertising as though they are speaking to colleagues.

Consumer values

Consumers value results and outcomes. They purchase products as a means to an end and want to know if your products will deliver the end result they are looking for.

Seller values

Sellers typically value their own brand, their own aspirations and their own incomes. Customers are simply a means to an end.

Two neighbourhoods

These two paradigms are like two neighbourhoods in which two communities live. Before you go looking for something to sell, you should get out of the sellers neighbourhood and into the buyers one. Here's what you should do:
Instead of asking what can I sell? You should ask, 'what do consumers want to buy?' Instead of asking what should I sell? You should ask, 'what are people buying?'

When you jump into the consumer world, you will be able to hear the conversation going on in their minds. Listen carefully until you can work out what are their main...

1. Issues
2. Concerns
3. Aspirations
4. Dreams
5. Fears
6. Desires
7. Doubts
8. Goals

These things will give you a clue as to what consumers want and therefore what you should sell.

When thinking of something to sell...

- Make sure that it plugs into the issues and aspirations of your consumers.
- Make sure that it is already in demand
- Make sure that it fits the customer's (self-seeking) paradigm
- Make sure that it speaks the customers (benefits based) language

- Make sure that it promises an outcome that is desirable to your customer.

The end result is that you will have found a 'buying market' with plenty of traffic (seekers).

Niche Marketing

So what is your prospective customer thinking right now? What are their issues and their concerns? The answer is that it all depends on which area of their life you are considering.

There are 8 major concerns for people living in the free world as follows:

1. **Spirituality:** This includes religion, philosophy, belief systems, guidance, inner peace, religious education, meditation, prayer and more.

2. **Health and fitness:** This includes medical issues, weight loss, physical fitness, mental health, wellness, nutrition and more

3. **Love and family:** This includes singles, dating, marriage, weddings, children, home improvements, schooling and more.

4. **Career:** This includes employment, career change, redundancy, rights, self-employment, business ownership and more.

5. **Personal finances:** This includes asset protection, wealth creation, debt, litigation, bankruptcy, savings, mortgages, financial services and more.

6. **Lifestyle:** This includes entertainment, friendships, hobbies, leisure, travel, music, social networking, nightlife and more.

7. **Personal development:** This includes self-education, reading, skills development, professional development, new languages, learning and growing and more.

8. **Contribution:** This includes charitable causes, public services, politics, associations, action groups, lobbying, fundraising and more.

These are the eight major concerns for people living in the free world.

*   **They also constitute eight market segments or sectors** for independent entrepreneurs.

*   **Each of these eight sectors houses hundreds of niche markets** for particular products or services.

*   **Each niche market houses thousands of micro-niche markets** for smart entrepreneurs. A micro niche is a niche within a niche.

For example, the personal development sector houses niche markets for various forms of skills training and success education. However within these markets there is a micro niche for success classics. i.e. success literature that is over 50 years old.

Likewise the **lifestyle sector** houses the **'hobbies niche.'** However within this niche is the **'model train micro-niche.'**

Stephen Pierce (an elite Internet Marketer) says, 'if you want to go broke, market to all the folk but if you want to get rich, then market to a niche.' (Pronounced 'nitch' in America)

The main thing to remember about any niche market is that consumers are never looking for products or services:

- They are looking for outcomes and results
- They are looking for a bargain
- They are looking for a risk free purchase (money back guarantee)
- They are looking for customer service

This way of thinking is critical for smart entrepreneurs who must decide what they are going to sell. If you answer this question in the customer's box, you are more likely to pick a niche that works.

Simply put yourself in the customer's shoes by jumping into one of the eight market segments and then ask yourself; 'what do I want to buy right now and why?' Imagine that you are a single parent then ask yourself; 'what do I want to buy right now?' Do the same for someone who is at risk of losing their job or for someone who is struggling to lose weight.

The critical skill

Thinking from the customer's perspective is a critical skill for independent entrepreneurs. That is why:

- You should work with a niche that you can relate to

- You should work with a niche that you have some knowledge of

- You should thoroughly research the niche to improve your knowledge of it.

- You should study the niche before sourcing a product

- You should obtain any available data about your niche before deciding to sell to it.

- You should find out what people really want (outcomes and results) in this field, so that you will know what to sell.

Why niche marketing works

The high street does not typically cater for special interests. It is designed for volume and so restricts its shop floors to items with broad appeal. **People with special interests have to search online for the few suppliers who can meet their specific requirements.** This is great news for independent entrepreneurs who are poised to meet the needs of macro and micro niche markets. Remember this: **Special needs require specialist services.**

Your self-concept

To be an effective independent entrepreneur you must learn to see yourself as a representative, a spokes-person and an advocate for your niche. There is an old and well-established war between the supply side of the market and the demand side as consumers have grown to mistrust companies and sales people. Sales people typically represent their companies and products but independent marketers typically represent their customers.

Representing your customers means:

- Appreciating their needs (in that area of their life)
- Appreciating their frustrations with existing products
- Appreciating their aspirations – the outcomes, results and objectives they really want.
- Appreciating their scepticism – mistrust of amazing offers!

If you can demonstrate an appreciation of your customers needs, frustrations, aspirations and scepticism, in your marketing documents (website, brochures, ads), you will achieve what I call **'customer rapport.'** Rapport could best be described as two people dancing to the same beat. When it is present, defences come down and the trust goes up.

Market research

This is why it is so critical that you research your market thoroughly so that you can acquaint yourself with consumer issues. Here's what you do:

Start by looking up hot trends around your subject of interest. Check out these sites to see what's hot and what's not!

www.amazon.com
www.google.com/trends
http://pulse.ebay.com/

These sites will tell you what's hot right now, what people are looking for right now and what people are buying right now!

- Join reputable online forums or discussions on your subject

- Subscribe to online newsletters on this subject
- Download any free e-books on your subject
- Try out your competitors to see what frustrates you
- Interview anyone you know who has a frustration in this area.
- Make a list of the 10 most common frustrations that people face in this area
- Find out how many searches are done per month around the key words in your niche market using Google ad words or similar tracking devices like **http://www.keywordspy.com** or **https://adwords.google.com/select/ KeywordToolExternal.**

A conflict of interests!

Sales people often experience a conflict of interests when pushing a product on customers that they neither want nor need. Since their chief aim is to sell the product and earn commissions, their approach can be intrusive. Authentic entrepreneurs on the other hand experience no such conflict because their chief aim is to satisfy, delight and even amaze their customers. They see themselves as customer representatives whose job it is to promote the best solutions for their customers needs. Their loyalties lie with the customer and not with their products.

In addition to this when it comes to Internet marketing, pushy sales tactics don't work because the customer has the power to silence you with the click of a mouse. They will only ever keep reading your website if you can achieve **'customer rapport.'**

Pitch your business in the future and stay ahead of the curve!

Anyone who can read trends can make money from home.
A trend is like traffic on the motorway; it's the direction in
which everything is moving. All you can do with a trend is,
get with it or get run over by it! So what are the key consumer
trends in today's world and how can you set up your business
so that all the traffic runs into it?

The first trend is bargains: People are looking for bargains
like never before. One of the things that the credit crunch
revealed is that everything was terribly over priced and that the
true value of stocks, property and services was much less than
advertised. Make sure that your business offers real bargains
to consumers and underground shoppers.

The second trend is cost-effectiveness: Anything that
can save me money is of interest to me. But I'm not odd;
companies and consumers alike feel the same way. With the
disappearance of easy credit has come the need for more cost
effective ways of getting things done. People want more for
less and are ready to pay anyone who can give it to them?
This is why the outsourcing business and cost saving
technology is booming!

**The third great trend is social networking and online
shopping:** People use the Internet to hunt for bargains,
to compare prices and to find specialist products. Online
shopping is on the up and up especially in a recession!
Face book has almost 500 million members. You Tube
likewise is slowly replacing Google as the search engine
of choice for hundreds of millions of people. Twitter and
My space are no different. This trend will continue to evolve.
My guess is that you will soon be able to buy products direct
from these sites.

The fourth great trend is home business opportunities:
People need more money - would you agree? A home business
is the most accessible and cost effective way to create
additional incomes. Many people have chosen it as their route
to financial independence and retirement! As the job market
shakes, more and more traffic will go down this lane.

The fifth great trend is the Green movement: Virtually
every product on planet earth is going to be replaced over
the next 100 years by an energy efficient and environmentally
friendly version of the same. Green products are in high
demand by companies and consumers alike who will have
to comply with increasing regulation and public pressure to
change their lifestyles. Like it or not, we are entering the
green revolution!

The sixth great trend is training and education: As the
world changes, it brings with it new technology, new rules and
new opportunities. Each of these will require new knowledge
and new skills from the masses. The hunger for information
will eventually become an international demand. Of course
governments will try to fill this gap, however people don't trust
governments like they use to and are always going to seek a
second opinion. This will make room for independents who can
package their training into audio, visual and literary products.

The seventh great trend is financial education: We don't
trust banks anymore and are more prone to read the small
print before signing any financial document. The group who
can translate financial jargon into everyday language will make
a fortune in the new world!

The eighth great trend is 'edutainment': No it's not a mis
spelling. The old learning styles are simply too boring for the
MTV generation. Learning must now be fun and entertaining.
We will see a fusion of comedy and learning, sports and

learning, music and learning, activities based learning and adventure-based learning.

Practice the I-STEP formula.

Nothing that you learn about running a home-based business will translate into cash unless you put it to work. You have to decide up front whether you want to learn for learning sake or whether you want to learn for earning sake. Once you decide that earning is the objective, you can practice this 5 part formula for success.

> **I = Innovation or Idea:** Ideas are the true source of wealth. Every multi-billion dollar organization started out as an idea in someone's mind. If you are serious about creating wealth, then you must first become serious about your own ideas. I recommend that you get an ideas book and make a note in it of every money-making idea that comes into your mind. Make sure that the book is of good quality and not a cheap scrapbook. The next step is to conduct some market research around those ideas to check that they are sound. At this stage however, all you have is a new idea!

> **S = Strategy:** The next task is to translate your idea into a plan of action. The best plans come complete with goals and targets, dates and deadlines, stages and steps. There are typically three stages to a good home business plan, namely, the set up, the launch and the growth stages. During the set up stage, you should list everything you need to have in place for a great launch. During the launch stage, you should design a campaign to build the expectation and

to make a bang. During the growth stage, you should plan an accelerated marketing campaign.

T = Test: Before launching your business, you should test every function of it thoroughly. You can do this with a few friends or simply run a pilot project. The goal here is to iron out the creases, perfect the process and optimize the outcomes. You want to feel confident that your business works. You also want to identify any errors in the system before you announce it to the world.

E = Execute: This means taking action and following through on your strategy. It basically means, do it! Set it up, launch it and grow it! Don't waste another minute. All your work will have been in vain if you don't take this critical step. It may seem daunting but if you complete the first three steps, you have nothing to lose and everything to gain.

P = Profits: The true test of a business innovation is how much extra cash it puts in your pocket. At this stage, you should review, measure and access your business venture in terms of hard cash. If it isn't making you any money, then something is wrong and it needs to be fixed immediately. If it is costing you more to run than you are making from it then slam on the breaks and change direction. You should keep tight financial records and review them regularly to see if you are still winning. A failure to review your own business can cost you years of wasted energy and missed opportunities.

Conclusion

A Matter Of Urgency!

The greatest transfer of wealth in the history of the world is going to take place over the next 3-5 years. Trillions are going to move away from the uninformed and towards the well informed. It will move from those playing the old game and towards those who are playing the new game and here's why:

1. THE JOBS ARE NOT COMING BACK – The millions of jobs that have been lost over the past two years in the private and public sectors are not going to return. Many of the roles are now obsolete and it is now much cheaper for companies to move their manufacturing off shore to an emerging economy where land and workers are much cheaper. Any published figures on unemployment do not include those who are under-employed. Those who have been forced into part-time work and the university graduates who are forced to work at Wal-Mart are not reflected in the figures. The true figures are gruesome and stand as absolute proof that the age of self-employment is here!

2. The public sector (government jobs) will continue to experience cuts and pay freezes as

governments struggle to reduce their deficits and to pay their debts. If America or the UK defaults on its debts, it may cause hyper-inflation in which the currencies will become worthless.

3. The bailouts and stimulus packages instituted by the governments of the free world have weakened the purchasing power of our currencies and will continue to do so for many years to come. Even though you will get less and less for your dollar as the years go by, wages are not going to rise to offset the affects of inflation. If you compare the price of a loaf of bread today versus 20 years ago, you will see how much value the dollar has lost in 20 years. Compare this with your pay scales and you will see that your wages have not increased in harmony with your cost of living.

4. The banking industry has not changed and will do everything in its power to recoup its losses. Banks make money through debt! Their dream scenario is to have every person and every company in the world indebted to them. They charge for the privilege of borrowing through interest and then retain a charge over your assets until the debt is paid. As an industry sector it will become more ruthless, more merciless and more aggressive in its attempts to make profits. We have already seen their losses passed on to the tax-payer through a series of bailouts and are about to see how ruthless the industry can be. In the first half of 2010, British banks received a record 1.3 million complaints from customers. This is a reflection of the

                    www.newgamerevolution.com

new face of banking. This will put pressure on individuals but more so on old-game industries who are out of sync with the new world!

Who pays the bill?

Guess who is going to pay for the government spending sprees and the corporate greed that led to millions of job losses and home repossessions in the free world? That's right, the old-gamers!

The job-dependent masses are going to be hit with inflation, hidden taxes, cuts in services and wage freezes in order to pay for the huge deficits of government and for the losses made by corporations through mismanagement and greed. This is just the beginning of the problem!

The real problem is the financial illiteracy and ignorance of the old gamers who are about to be robbed in broad daylight. You see there are two sets of rules governing the financial world. One set for the uninformed and another for the well-informed. The financially mis-informed are those who think that things will swing back to where they were. Jobs will become available and banks will lend freely again. They think that their savings and policies will be enough to support them through retirement. Some even believe that a State pension will keep them for life. This may have been true for some in the past but it will not be true in the future.

The future belongs to the entrepreneurs who know how to locate or to create alternative sources of income. The new **GAME** is about **Generating Alternative Money-sources as an Entrepreneur!**

It is the game you must master and win if you are going to survive the systematic collapse of the old economic era.

This recession is like a wedge that is being driven into the job-dependent middle classes. It is forcing them in one of two directions. They will either become very poor or they will become very rich. Those who become very poor will not do so for lack of opportunity. They will be destroyed for lack of knowledge.

You will literally have to become a self-motivated, self-managed and self-determined entrepreneur in order to get on the winning side of the wedge.

The messianic complex of the old-gamers!

Most hope that a politician will save them. They actually believe that there are two parties out there fighting for office and that one will save them while the other will make things worse. This is an illusion that the mis-educated masses have embraced as a fact.

Don't get me wrong, I'm all for voting, however I think that political illiteracy is at the heart of our political frustrations and disillusionments. We have to be realistic about what a government can do to change our financial situation.

They can please some of the people some of the time, but they cannot please all of the people all of the time. They are in debt and their options are seriously limited. Their strategies and solutions can only involve a combination of three things, any one of which will make them unpopular. They may cut services, increase taxes or dilute the currency by printing more money.

When a politician promises to reduce taxes, what they are really saying is that they are going to make cuts in public spending. This makes them unpopular with those who are State-dependent. When they say that they are going to improve or reform public services, what they are really saying is that they are going to raise taxes.

This makes them unpopular with taxpayers. When they say that they wish to stimulate the economy with a cash injection, what they are really saying is that they are going to print money out of thin air or that they are going to borrow it and then pass the debt on to you. This will diminish the purchasing power of your currency.

This is all you can expect, in one form or another, from any government in the modern world. The answer does not lie with government; it lies with you!

Your locus of control!

In psychology there is the theory called 'The locus of control.' This theory says that people, who believe that they are victims of external forces or that factors outside of themselves will determine what becomes of them, have an external 'locus of control.' These people are most likely to suffer from mental illness in the form of chronic anxiety, paranoia, depression and psychosis. On the other hand those who take responsibility for their own conditions and who believe that they can do something about their own circumstances, have an internal 'locus of control.' These are most likely to survive turbulent times with their mental health intact.

Where is your locus of control? If you are waiting for a political party to take us back to the days of job-security then you may end up losing the plot both financially and mentally. If on the other hand you realize that your financial future is in your own hands and that you can create the security you need as an independent entrepreneur, then this crisis will quickly become your opportunity!

Making the transition

The transition from an employee to an entrepreneur is fundamentally a psychological one. You literally have to stop thinking like an employee and start thinking like an entrepreneur.

Employees work for wages, but entrepreneurs work for profits. Employees trade time for money, but entrepreneurs trade ideas for money. Employees work for money, but entrepreneurs work to create money sources. These differences are psychological in nature and they work best for people with a positive mental attitude.

This sort of paradigm shift doesn't happen over night. That is why I advise you to start your entrepreneurial journey with a year of self-development. During this time you should immerse yourself into the world of positive thinking and success psychology. I highly recommend the following books, even though some of them are old, they continue to be a source of inspiration and transformation for people who read them today:

1. **Think and Grow Rich** – Napoleon Hill

2. **As a man thinketh** – James Allen

3. **The magic of thinking big** – David Schwartz

4. **The power of positive thinking** – Norman V Peel

5. **The power of focus** – Mark Victor Hansen

6. **Multiple streams of income** – James Allen

7. **Rich dad, poor dad** – Robert Kiyosaki

8. **The cash-flow quadrant** – Robert Kiyosaki

9. **The Strangest Secret** – Earl Nightingale

10. **Live your dream** – Les Brown

11. **Wake up the giant within** – Tony Robbins

12. **Getting rich** – Brian Tracy

Tools for transformation

Knowledge and skills are the tools of the 21st century. This means if you can identify your own knowledge gaps and skills deficiencies, then you are very likely to succeed in business. Simply decide to learn anything that you need to know in order to achieve the goals that you set for yourself.

Likewise you should realize that skills can be learned, developed and mastered. Consider this simple fact: everyone who is at the top of his or her field right now was once at the bottom. Every master can remember a time when the thought of doing, what today seems so natural, use to terrify them. They got better and better through trial and error and so can you!

Leadership is a skill, so is marketing, sales, negotiation and project management. Since these are skills, then they can be learned and developed by anyone. Decide to develop a wide range of business and leadership skills. These will serve you well when you finally begin trading.

The choice is simple!

The choice set before you is quite simple: play the old game by giving 40 years of your life to an employer in exchange for just enough to pay your bills or join the new game revolution by creating multiple money sources as an independent entrepreneur. The old game means relying a solo income from a job that could go at any minute with little or no notice.

It also means borrowing your success through loans, overdrafts, credit and store cards on the strength of an unsecured job.

This game worked for many in the past but will not work for you in the future.

The new game is all about multiple incomes from numerous ventures. Initially this may start out as a part-time hobby but eventually it has the potential to make you financially secure and free.

A better future

We all want a better future for ourselves and for loved ones.

The first question is: will you create it or will you wait for someone else to create it for you? The greatest transfer of wealth in the history of the world is going to take money away from those who are waiting for it to happen and transfer it to those who are making it happen. Money will move from the passive and move towards the proactive. It will leave the uninformed and cleave to the well informed. The main job is to create the future of your dreams.

The second question is: will you build your future on the fault line of job-security or will you build it on the bedrock of entrepreneurship? The idea of Job-security is the fault line at the heart of the eco-quake that has devastated the incomes, the homes and the dreams of millions of old-gamers! However a crisis is always the birth of a new season. In the after math of the quake it would be foolish to build along the same fault lines. It makes sense to embrace a new strategy for success; one that is based on the fundamental law of economics, namely, the law of supply and demand. The new game is a strategy that is based on innovation, trade and service to others.

The final question is: Will you start now or will you procrastinate and wait till it's too late? You can start right now by joining the New Game Revolution at www.newgamerevoluton.com for more information and support as you embark on your year of transformation.

May this book become the catalyst that kick starts your own four-year plan to become an independent entrepreneur or a virtual millionaire from your own multiple sources of income!